HUNCOAT UNCOATED

(Life and Past Times in Huncoat)

by

John Goddard

Landy Publishing
2004

ISBN 1 872895 64 6

British Library in Cataloguing Publication Data.
A catalogue record of this book is available from the British Library.

Layout by Mike Clarke. *Tel/Fax: 01254 395848*
Printed by Nayler the Printer Ltd., Accrington. *Tel: 01254 234247*

Landy Publishing have also published:

Accrington's Changing Face by Frank Watson & Bob Dobson
Accrington's Public Transport 1886-1986 by Robert Rush
Oswaldtwistle Observed: Gawping at Gobbinland by Mike Booth and Albert Wilkinson
Blackburn Tram Rides by Jim Halsall
Blackburn in Focus by Alan Duckworth & Jim Halsall
Preston in Focus by Stephen Sartin
Bolland Forest & the Hodder Valley by Greenwood & Bolton
A Preston Mixture edited by Bob Dobson
A Blackburn Miscellany edited by Bob Dobson

A full list is available from:

Landy Publishing
'Acorns' 3 Staining Rise, Staining, Blackpool, FY3 0BU
Tel/Fax: 01253 895678
e-mail: bobdobson@amserve.co.uk

INTRODUCTION

Apart from being an obvious play on words, the title of this book also describes its purpose; to uncover something of the history and development of the village over the thousand years or so of its existence.

Other authors, notably Richard Ainsworth and John Smith, have recorded some of its history and others have dealt with individual families or village institutions. All of these publications are now scarce and only available second-hand. Ainsworth's and Smith's books were written more than seventy years ago and the village has seen immense changes in that time. This book is an attempt to bring the story of Huncoat up-to-date.

My title also refers, tongue in cheek, to a so-called tradition still occasionally repeated, that the village owes its name to an incident during the Civil War. In late November 1642 a force of Parliamentary supporters assembled on the Altham side of Whinney Hill to oppose a Royalist advance from Blackburn through Enfield. The story goes that before the fight the local lads were told to *get yer jackets off and get stuck in'*. But, being an army, the command was given in the military fashion of *'Squaaaaad – wait for it – squad uncoat'*. So they became Uncoaters! No doubt some gullible outsider wouldn't realise he was having his leg pulled. It's our hope that Huncoaters old and new, near and far, will find much to interest and inform them, re-awaken memories and encourage a pride in the township to which they belong.

I am indebted to many people who have ensured that records and photographs of old Huncoat have been preserved. My special thanks go to Lancashire Library, especially Helen Barrett and Cath Duckworth of Accrington Local Studies Library, Jim Ashton, Albert & Marjorie Blackburn, Mary Swindells, Bob Rush, Garth Dawson, St Augustine's Church, Frank Whewell, the late Dorothy Jaques and the late Jim Leitherd, all of whom have given generously of their time and memories or permitted the use of photographs. Bob Dobson added some final suggestions, and Mike Clarke has transformed my rough layout into a polished publication. Without their help this book would not have been possible.

John C Goddard
Huncoat 2004

Origins

The earliest written record of the name *Huncoat* occurs in the survey of England ordered by William the Conqueror and produced in 1086. This census of the nation's landholders and its wealth has become known to generations of Englishmen as the *Domesday Book*. In highly abbreviated Latin it records that Huncoat was one of only five places mentioned by name in the whole of Blackburn Hundred, an area which equates to present day north east Lancashire, stretching south and east of the River Ribble to the Rossendale Valley and the Yorkshire border.

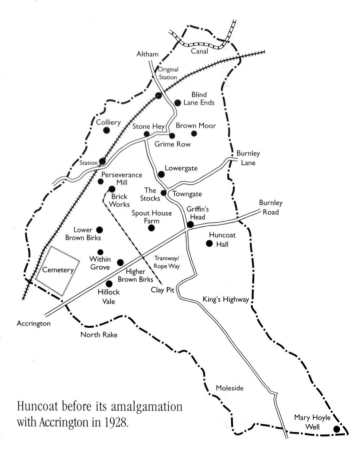

Translation:

In the same Hundred [in 1066] King Edward had Hunnicot with two carucates [of land]/ Walton with two carucates/ Pendleton with half a hide.

But the name itself tells us that the village is of Anglo-Saxon origin and gives an indication of the occupation of the first settlers. Most authorities say that Hun or Hunna is a personal name, although another suggestion is that it may refer to honey. Cote is an Old English name for a shelter for small animals. The same sense occurs in dovecote, hencote and pigeoncote and there is a Sheepcotes farm in Accrington. It is more frequently found as a name element in the Midlands. Incidentally, the present spelling of the name seems to date only from the middle of the 1800s. Could it have been that some outsider misspelt what he heard?

The township occupies the high ground on the south of the Calder valley where settlements were established early in the Anglo-Saxon period. So it seems likely that Huncoat originated, after the more fertile land in the valley bottom was already taken, as the smallholding of a later English settler, keeping sheep, goats or bees and growing enough crops to be self-sufficient.

Huncoat before its amalgamation with Accrington in 1928.

Left: The boundaries of the township, dividing it from Altham, Hapton and Accrington, were established well before 1066. On the Accrington side the boundary started from a point on the slopes of Hameldon near Mary Hoyle Well and crossed Moleside towards the steep drop of North Rake above Burnley Road. At some point along the moor was a boundary marker described in the 13th century as *'the pointed stone in Fernihalgh'*. This stone was still in place until the early 20th century and is shown here propped up by Arthur Ainsworth.

Below: At the edge of North Rake the boundary followed the stream down the clough, through Within Grove to eventually join the river Calder at Altham. In the 19th century the stream was diverted into the Burnley Road reservoir but a part known as *Tom Brook* can still be seen near Marl House on Enfield Road.

In the 12th century, when monks from Kirkstall Abbey surveyed their property in Accrington, the clough was called *Wormley Clough*. The name is not marked on any maps but it survived in a very corrupt version as *Warm Leaf*, a farm opposite Hillock Vale, now part of the cemetery

Above: On the Hapton side the boundary followed the western edge of Cronker Clough and continued down the valley along the line of the A56 road where it drops to meet the M65 motorway below Burnley Road.

The northern boundary with Altham is not as markedly distinct but ran along a line roughly east to west between the canal and the M65 motorway.

Right: Although the township has lost its former independent status these boundaries have remained virtually unchanged for ten centuries, having survived several changes of local government control in that time.

Some minor gains and losses have taken place. Before 1928 the boundary with Accrington was at Whitewell Road, a few hundred yards further west of the ancient line. This sign was one of several to be found on the boundaries of Accrington at that time.

A Farming Community

For most of its existence Huncoat has been a farming community and remnants are still carried on at the beginning of the twenty-first century. In 1901 the census listed 25 farms. In 2004 only four still carry on some remnant of agricultural activity, six are private houses and fifteen have been demolished.

For the first few centuries of the medieval period there are very few documents referring to Huncoat. The few records that do exist show that the villagers were a self-contained and largely self-sufficient community, existing on the produce of their farms for food and clothing and using local natural materials for building and fuel.

At the end of the thirteenth century the audited accounts of the De Lacy estates in the area reveal the types of farming activity taking place in Accrington district. Crops of corn, oats and flax were grown and the corn mill in Accrington was in operation. Land was being cleared, drained and hedged. Oxen rather than horses were used to pull ploughs and carts. Cattle were being raised, the milk made into butter and cheese, the hides tanned for leather. In summer the meadows were mown and the hay stored for winter feed. Strangely there is no mention of sheep or pigs but undoubtedly these would also be kept for meat and wool. The only mention of Huncoat in the accounts is that the De Lacys received £5.05 in rents from the township. This seems to indicate that the inhabitants of Huncoat were left to manage their own farms so long as they paid their rents and the other customary dues for which they were liable. Another document of 1311 shows that Huncoat tenants farmed a total of 309 acres and paid their rent annually at the Feast of St Giles (Sept. 1st). The total acreage of the township has always been more than 900 acres so much of the land at this time was commons or waste.

The nineteenth century saw a gradual change to dairy farming, coinciding with the rapid growth of Accrington. By the end of the century farmers were making a prosperous living by concentrating on haymaking and milk production. In mid-century the milk was conveyed in wheel-barrows along the newly made Burnley Road, later by donkeys with panniers and ended up with more than twenty horse-drawn milk floats trundling down to Accrington every morning. Not everyone welcomed these farmers their prosperity. Some villagers grumbled because farms got a 50% discount on their rates.

Above: Huncoat Hall is the largest farm in the township and the one with the longest recorded history. In 1316 John de Huncoat exchanged his lands for those of William Birtwistle of Bradley in Hapton. The descendents of William Birtwistle remained in Huncoat for almost 500 years at Huncoat Hall and the Old Hall. Their fortunes fluctuated through the centuries from being granted a coat of arms in 1560 to near bankruptcy in the 18th century.

 After the Birtwistles, the hall was at one time divided into five dwellings and was later acquired by the Towneley family, who carried out major alterations. Some features of the medieval hall remain and Pevsner, in his 'Buildings of England', suggested that an investigation of these features is needed.

Right: The name Birtwistle comes from an ancient farm or estate in Hapton whose exact whereabouts are lost. As a surname it dates back to the 1200s and is widespread throughout the area. Conversely the name Huncoat seems never to have been adopted as a surname. This coat of arms was granted to Oliver Birtwistle of Huncoat Hall in 1560, the second year of Queen Elizabeth 1. The stone was over the door of Old Hall farm and was salvaged when that building was demolished. It is now built into a retaining wall facing Burnley Lane with an explanatory plaque.

Left and below: In 1390 the rent for one eighth part of Brown Moor farm was a half penny or a pair of gloves. A document dated 1495 names Brown Moor in the ownership of Lettice, wife of Nicholas Towneley. At the time of the Civil War it was the home of the Bentley family who combined farming with shoemaking. William Bentley was paid for binding a book in 1748 and Edward Bentley was the head of the family in 1881. A daughter of his married John Hudson and they took over the farm. Their descendents still live in the village where a millstone from the farm preserves the name. The farm buildings were demolished in 1948 to make way for the construction of the power station.

Bottom: The lane through Brown Moor farmyard carried on to Brick Barn on the Hapton boundary. Its sole claim to distinction was that it was the only old building not built in stone

The huddle of farms and barns which comprise the Hillhouse group are much altered but keep the typical pattern of a hamlet surrounded by fields enclosed in ancient times. The inn and stocks complete the scene which, whilst not a picture postcard English village, reflects the grittier nature of upland Lancashire.

In 1425 Richard of Hillhouse was fined 1s.4d for chasing a neighbour's sheep to death. Was this through drunken high spirits or an early example of a neighbour from hell? Whatever the reason it shows that Hillhouse has a long history. The existing building is not quite so old but it is the oldest intact farmhouse in the village, dating to around 1600. Many villagers remember buying Birtwell's home-made ice cream there, with *'dragon's blood'* topping if you wanted. The old barn nearby was replaced in 1990 by two houses on the site. They were named *'Pipers Row'* after a row of cottages with the same name which stood close by until 1900.

Middle Hillhouse was a typical local farm-house of the 1730s when several other Huncoat farms were built or rebuilt. The house and barn have been demolished in January 2004, to be replaced by new houses.

Lower Hill House barn before conversion.

Lower Hillhouse presents the architectural fashion of the later 1700s with higher rooms and larger windows influenced by the Georgian style. It may have replaced an earlier building since the Birtwistle family sold a farm known as *Lower House* in 1741.

Left and bottom right: Lower and Higher Brown Birks farms are recorded in the 1550s and are probably much older, though the buildings shown are of a later date.

Although all Huncoat farms have proper names they have usually been known locally by the names of their occupiers. Hence old residents referred to Lower Brown Birks (pictured right) as *Newhouse's* farm and slightly younger ones to it as *Whewell's*.

Left centre: Jim Whewell happily goes about his work on the Fordson tractor. Behind him is a glimpse of the wartime prefabricated houses which got the nickname *'Sawdust City'* because of the insulation in the wall panels. These were eventually replaced by the Burnley Road flats and other council houses

Below left: In the 1950s Lower Brown Birks farm was acquired by Manchester Corporation as a construction site and access point for the tunnelling of the Haweswater aqueduct which brought piped water from the Lake District to Manchester.

In 1958 the farm was bought by Accrington Corporation who demolished it to extend Bolton Avenue to the industrial estate. The semi-detached houses of Haweswater Road were built for the site managers of the tunnelling scheme.

Halfway between Stone Hey and the station stood Broad Meadows farm. In the 1840s a day school was started here by William Herd, the former Baptist pastor, despite him having been accused of being *'a poor, illiterate, former weaver'*.

The lane alongside crossed over the railway and into the pit-head buildings, where the chimneys of the coke ovens tower above the roof. The adjacent barn was demolished to widen Station Road in the 1930s.

Below: Along Altham Lane from Stone Hey were two farms known as *Blind Lane Ends*. These two undistinguished farm buildings suffered the same fate as Brown Moor, having stood about where the future entrance to the power station was to be.

Packhorse Track to Motorway

Huncoat village is built at the crossroads of two ancient tracks. Both date at least from early medieval times and may have existed before 1066. One comes over the moors from Rossendale and continues through Altham over the Nick o' Pendle to Clitheroe, the Lancashire HQ of the Lord of the Manor. Its name, *the King's Highway*, reflects this use, although the Lord of the Manor was at various times an Earl, the King and a Duke. The other runs east to west from Burnley to Blackburn connecting several small townships on the way. These major routes, little more than cart tracks, were supplemented by paths connecting the local farms to each other and to the main tracks. Most of the older roads in Huncoat are called *'lanes'*; Burnley, Spout House, Brownbirks, Blind, Bull, Fish, Scatchen. The three exceptions are Highergate, Lowergate and the now disappeared Millgate, which all retain the Norse word *'gata'* meaning a road or way. Recent times have added another *'road'* to the name so we now have *'higher road road'* and *'lower road road'*.

These old roads, badly maintained and only suitable for pedestrians and horses, were hopelessly inadequate by the late 1700s. Large industrial concerns were producing increased quantities of consumer goods for national markets and required more efficient transport. One early solution was the canal system. In 1801 the Leeds & Liverpool Canal skirted the northern boundary of Huncoat but only a very short stretch was actually in the township. Although there was some passenger traffic from Altham Barn bridge the canal had little effect on development in Huncoat.

Greater benefit came when the present Burnley Road was built in the mid 1830s. This followed a more direct line than the old track through Castle Clough and an easier gradient in the dip below Huncoat Hall, by-passing the village centre. Earlier still in the 1780s the King's Highway route had been replaced by the present Manchester to Whalley Road through Accrington, an indication of the growing importance of that town.

Still more significant for Huncoat was the East Lancashire Railway. This opened in 1848 and ran through the township with a station only a cockstride from the village centre. The railway attracted most of the early 20th century industrial development in Huncoat.

Even with these improvements most Huncoat residents still had to walk on local journeys. It wasn't until 1907 that they could catch a tram into Accrington, and even then had to go to Hillock Vale to get on. There wasn't a bus service into the village until 1928.

By the 1970s industrial goods traffic had either disappeared from Huncoat or was being carried by road. The railway station is now used only by passenger traffic and the canal is devoted to pleasure boats. Increasing road use, by private motorists and the haulage industry, has added another layer of road building in the 1980s and has put Huncoat firmly in the midst of the national motorway network, although problems of access to the local industrial estates and waste disposal site remain to be solved.

Above: The King's Highway across Moleside. John Wesley travelled from Padiham to Haslingden in 1788 and denounced the moorland roads as *'enough to lame my horse and shake any carriage to pieces'*. He vowed never to use them again but he was 85 years old at the time so it wasn't very likely anyway. Two hundred years later construction of the Accrington easterly bypass (A56) closely followed the same line across the moor and down through the former quarry.

When Burnley Road was built in 1835 it cut past the village and crossed the King's Highway in the dip below Huncoat Hall. All new roads need *'service stations'* for travellers so before 1839 Shaw's Blackburn Brewery had built an inn with John Harrison as the landlord, perhaps one of their first houses outside Blackburn. It faced away from the old highway which then became of secondary importance. In the 1841 census it is listed as Cross Gates because of its position at the crossroads. It had been renamed the *Griffin's Head* before the next census in 1851.

At about the same time, a mile or so further down the road, another *'service station'* was built where Burnley Road crossed the boundary into Accrington. This too was at a crossroads, where an old track went to Hillock Bank at the foot of the Coppice and down into Accrington. The inn took its name from the Whitaker family of Simonstone who owned the land. Generations of local people have known it as the *Cemetery Hotel* before it reverted to its original name of *Whitakers Arms* in 1997. It advertises *'Good stabling'* and *'Bowling Green'*. Just behind were some buildings known as *Woodnook Farm* with a datestone of 1756.

On the crest of the road as it went from the *Griffin's Head* into the village stood Old Hall Farm bearing the coat-of-arms of the Birtwistle family and the date 1768. Dorothy Birtwistle, daughter of Oliver of Huncoat Hall, married Daniel Barrowclough in 1749. Their names are carved on the datestone which can still be seen in the village.

All the old tracks converged in Towngate, the centre of the village. Lawrence Rawcliffe built the *White Lion* in about 1780 and it became the social and commercial centre of village life before there were any religious bodies to provide competition for social activities. As well as providing accommodation and sustenance, clubs met there, auctions took place and news and gossip was passed on. Much of the old property in the background has now been demolished and the same view now is much more open and less grim.

What is now called *'anti-social behaviour'* was once punished by offenders being put in the stocks where they could be seen by everyone – the old way of *naming and shaming!* Where else would be the most appropriate place except opposite the pub? The stocks have been moved and restored several times but have been recognised as part of Huncoat's heritage since they were railed round in about 1906.

Bottom right: One of the uprights bears the date 1722 and has also been used as a signpost. The stone is very worn but on one side can be made out – To Blackburn – To Burnley. On another side is – To Haslingden. Curiously this direction has the letters carved right to left, as if the mason was writing the way the road was pointing.

Burnley Lane is the old road from Hapton into Towngate. When this photograph was taken around 1900 there were only a few separate groups of cottages on the lane, occupied by miners, weavers and a few shopkeepers. These still survive and were soon joined by rows of terraced houses.

Above: One of the older shops with a raised loading platform in front was at No. 5 and had been a 'putting-out shop' where handloom weavers collected yarn and delivered woven cloth.

Right: No.16 was a grocery shop before the First World War. Both are now converted into houses.

Across from the *White Lion* and behind the stocks, Spout House Lane was one of the roads to Accrington. Before the railway was built James Allen farmed Spout House and also ran coaches to Burnley, Blackburn and Blackpool through Altham and Enfield. The horses were changed at the Walton Arms and brought up to Spout House to rest in stables that James Allen built on Burnley Road opposite Rockdale. Later the Clegg family lived here for a hundred years with the result that the lane became known as *Clegg's Lane*.

When these Edwardian chapelgoers had their annual procession it was wide enough to accommodate their hats! Today it is overgrown but still used.

The old highway continued out of Towngate, passing the lamp and Nos. 10 and 11 Highergate. These two cottages were demolished to make it easier for the bus to negotiate the sharp and narrow bend past Howard's Farm with its pediment dated 1866. Behind Lower Hill House barn it curved in front of Ormerod Row to come out opposite the *Black Bull* at Lowergate. Ormerod Row backed onto a field and the *'necessary offices'*, i.e. privies, were across the lane. The public conveniences had a short life in the 1950s. This narrow and twisty old road through the village was widened and straightened between the two world wars when Lowergate Road cut through to the *Black Bull*.

Above: The rear of Ormerod Row with the public conveniences on the right.

Right: Howard's or Highergate Farm shortly before its demolition in the 1960s.

The *Black Bull* is probably the oldest of the five hostelries in Huncoat, with humble beginnings as a house selling beer. Until 1871 the census returns list it simply as one of the cottages at Lowergate or Cornmarket with the occupier being a beerseller rather than an innkeeper and so not allowed to sell wines and spirits. In 1881 it is named as the *Black Bull beerhouse,* its name reflecting its connection with farming – the only one of the five village pubs to do so.

Forming an open square behind the pub was a group of 18th century cottages known as *Cornmarket.* The name suggests that local farmers met here to buy and sell produce and animals. They would naturally need a pint or more of home brew after some hard bargaining!

The site is now a car park for the pub and, very appropriately, what was once the corn market is now used by the mobile chiropody clinic for its regular visits.

At the *'Bull'* a choice of routes was available. Off to the left, Fish Lane, officially gentrified to Lynwood Road in 1933, went past Fish House farm and led into Scatchen Lane over Whinney Hill to Church or joined a lane across the fields to Brown Birks. Fish House farm is probably named after a family of that name. A Robert Fish is recorded as living in Huncoat in 1563 and William Fish was the churchwarden for Huncoat in 1751.

Straight ahead the lane dropped down the hill to Stone Hey where it veered right to Altham. Now known as Lowergate Road it has also been known locally as *Bull Lane* and *Co-op Lane*, possibly depending on whether you were going up to the Bull or down to the Co-op. In the distance are the factory chimneys of Altham Brick and Tile Works alongside the canal. The firm operated from about 1890 until World War One .

Above: At the junction with Station Road the stone cottages comprising Stone Hey farm and out-buildings have been concealed with mock Tudor timbering. In the barn a date of 1738 and the initials of Richard and Ellen Fort are carved on a beam. Their son, also Richard, invested in the early calico printing works at Broad Oak and Oakenshaw. He later built Highbrake House and rebuilt Read Hall where he lived in the early 1800s. Stone Hey was later farmed by James Pollard who was also parish clerk of Altham for 35 years. His son John built the adjacent terrace of houses dated 1859

Left: Further along Altham Lane the road went to Grime Row before taking a sharp turn left down the hill. The name has nothing to do with dirt but, because it appears to have, the restored and improved cottages were re-named Peter Grime Row in 1978. Why Peter was chosen is a mystery. William 'Billy' Grime lived there in the mid 1800s and there is no Peter Grime in the village censuses. Perhaps it was mistaken from the opera of similar name by Benjamin Britten!

In the mid 1840s gangs of labourers were at work in Huncoat constructing the embankments, cuttings and bridges for the East Lancashire Railway line which cut through several farmlands and the grounds of Highbrake House. At the end of May 1848 an experimental run was made from Accrington to Bentley Wood and the line opened to the public in September. Maps of the time show that the first station was on Altham Lane but before long it was moved to the mill side of the level crossing. A local petition in 1881 complained about the *'disgraceful accommodation'*. The photograph shows the station as rebuilt in 1912. The buildings consisted of a lamp room, outside men's lavatory, a porter's room, a ladies' waiting room with inside toilets, the booking and parcel office and a general waiting room.

Until the 1940s the station was very busy with goods traffic from the mill, the brickworks and the extensive sidings serving the colliery, so busy that it won an award for the tonnage handled by the station. Now the station could more properly be called a *'halt'* – the only accommodation being a bus type shelter on the exposed platform.

ELEVATION TO MAIN LINE.

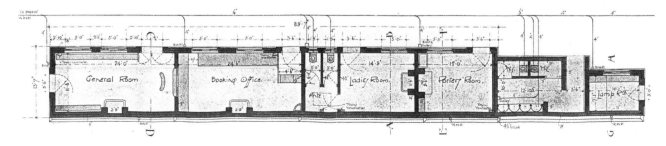

Horse and cart, the *'iron horse'* and *'shanks's pony'* remained the only means of transport in the village for another eighty years after the railway. Accrington Corporation began to run trams along Burnley Road in 1907 but the terminus was at Hillock Vale, (shown here) only just inside the Huncoat boundary. Beyond that there were not enough prospective passengers for the line to be economic. The first World War stopped any discussion of extending the tramway into the village and the last tram ran on the Burnley Road section in 1932.

One of the incentives for Huncoat to amalgamate with Accrington was the promise to provide a bus service. The Huncoat route was one of the first to open in November 1928 before the take-over became official in 1929. This 18 seat Dennis single decker passing the Black Bull was painted in a new livery, the dark blue and red familiar to later generations of bus users. It is thought that these colours, used by the East Lancashire Regiment, along with black-edged windows, were a mark of respect to the *'Accrington Pals'*.

Once the bus service started it became obvious that the narrow roads and sharp bends in the village were difficult to negotiate. So throughout the 1930s Accrington Corporation carried out a programme of widening and straightening the road from the *Griffin* to the station. After the war the building of Within Grove housing estate required Brownbirks Lane to be re-made and it was re-named *Bolton Avenue* in 1948.

With small alterations the road pattern in the village remains the same as it has been for centuries. But along the eastern and northwestern boundaries major new roads have transformed access from Huncoat to the rest of Britain — or perhaps vice versa!

The A56 trunk road, re-routed from the Rossendale side of Hameldon in 1986, links the M65 Calder Valley motorway with the M66 to Manchester. Its northern section is shown here in 1983 when it stopped suddenly at Burnley Road.

Industrial Huncoat

The Industrial Revolution arrived late in Huncoat and disappeared relatively quickly. The lack of a water supply sufficient to power a mill delayed the detrimental effects of manufacturing until the middle of the nineteenth century. Another factor may be that the major landholders were the Towneley and Whitaker families; landed gentry rather than the upwardly mobile entrepreneurs of other towns. The village was not overwhelmed by mills and housing until much later than its neighbours and retained its rural aspect throughout the hundred or so years when its economy was mainly dependent on cotton and coal.

There had always been some small-scale industrial activity to supplement farm incomes and for personal needs. Natural resources of stone and coal were quarried and mined for building and heating. Handloom weaving of wool, and later cotton, in farmhouses and cottages was highly organised by the eighteenth century with a distribution system through merchants and markets.

In the second quarter of the nineteenth century, the ancient and badly maintained trackways were being replaced by turnpike roads, and the railway network was rapidly being extended, reaching Huncoat in 1848.

These developments in communications and the availability of steam power led to the building of two mills in the township, followed in the late 1880s by the colliery and, soon after, the brickworks. Between 1851 and 1861 the population of Huncoat increased by 40% as workers were attracted to the mills, many of them coming from northern Ribblesdale, especially from the area around Settle. The nineteenth century census returns record that the residents of Huncoat were almost entirely manual workers, labouring on the land, in the mines or in the mills.

But in little more than a hundred years these extractive and manufacturing industries had disappeared from the township except for some quarrying of clay for brickmaking. A new wave of industrial development began with the acquisition in 1957 by Accrington Corporation of land between the railway and Whinney Hill for an industrial estate. Several anxious years followed until firms began to move on to the estate in the 1970s and the confidence of the Council was justified. A mixture of national and local, large and small, manufacturing and service industries now operate from Huncoat.

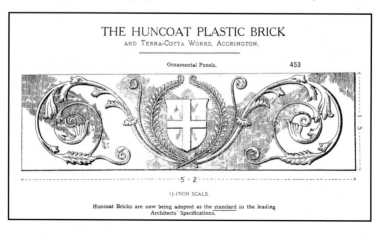

THE HUNCOAT PLASTIC BRICK
AND TERRA-COTTA WORKS, ACCRINGTON.

Ornamental Panels. 453

5' - 2"

1½-INCH SCALE.

Huncoat Bricks are now being adopted as the standard in the leading Architects' Specifications.

This aerial view shows the lower part of the village in its industrial heyday between the two world wars. At the bottom are the extensive brickworks with the old quarry and the conveyor bringing shale from the later quarries above Burnley Road. Between the works and the railway is Highbrake Mill with its weaving shed and four storey spinning mill. To the right of the mill is the crescent of Highbrake and Prospect Terraces and the Railway Hotel at the end of Station Road. Across the railway are the row of coke ovens and sidings of the pit with lines of coal waggons. The embankment and viaduct carry the light railway which linked Whinney Hill brickworks and Moorfield Colliery to the main line. Lack of smoke from the many chimneys indicates that the photograph was perhaps taken one afternoon in the Wakes Week, otherwise one can almost smell the air pollution and hear the racket of this busy scene.

In 1853 two mills were being built in Huncoat. Perseverance Mill, more commonly called *Highbrake Mill,* was a cotton spinning and weaving mill built by John S Grimshaw alongside the railway near the present station. John Grimshaw built Woodside House in 1862 and lived there until he retired to St Annes. He was very active on the parish council and other local public offices. From 1874 the mill passed through several ownerships until bought by John Barnes in 1899. To celebrate the marriage of his daughter about 1910 he treated 253 workpeople plus friends to a trip to Blackpool, paying their railway fare and giving them 1s 6d (7.5p) each for tea.

The mill closed down in 1941 and didn't re-open after the war. It became derelict and was demolished in 1954, with only some foundations remaining. Early in 2004 the site was completely cleared for a new housing estate but the stone chimney base has been retained.

John Barnes

The other mill, at Hillock Vale, was a weaving shed built by Shutt Bros. and later owned by J. S. Grimshaw who leased the premises to several firms. The weaving shed was demolished in 1926 and Hillock Vale garage built on the site. A fire destroyed the remaining buildings in 1930.

One side of the mill was overlooked by the embankment of Burnley Road reservoir which was drained in the 1980s and later replaced by Foxwood Chase housing estate.

On the other side, Vale Court, South Street and Parker Street were built to house the workers at the mill. This little community had its corner shop, was close to the pub and built its own air raid shelter at the outbreak of World War Two.

Parker Street is the only part remaining. A group of Anglicans meeting at No.2 Parker Street were the impetus for the creation of St Augustine's mission in 1886.

Hillock Vale frontage to Burnley Road. The tramlines and two of the cast iron poles which carried the overhead electric tram wires date the picture to after 1907. The archway leads into Vale Court and on the right is the corner shop with a postbox. Early photographs always attracted a crowd of youngsters. Some of these are old enough to have been working half-time at the mill but they seem too neatly turned out for it to be a weekday. The boys in particular could almost be in uniform with their knee britches, Eton collars, caps and polished clogs. The village bobby, who almost always appears in old photographs, is noticeably absent on this occasion – just when crowd control is needed – and he only lived just up the road!

Unusually for the period, the Hillock Vale houses were built of brick, made on site by James Ashworth in a temporary brickworks.

Large scale brickmaking started in 1894 when Huncoat brickworks began operations near the station using the trade mark *'Redac'* for red Accrington brick. The original quarry was behind the works but later shale was brought from a new quarry above Burnley Road. A tramway carried the tubs of shale through a tunnel under Burnley Road but after a fatal accident to the village policeman's daughter this was replaced by an overhead cable system that became a widely-known landmark. This was dismantled in the 1960s and the brickworks itself closed down at the end of 1992.

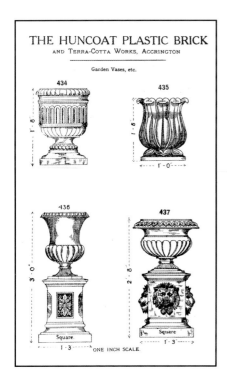

THE HUNCOAT PLASTIC BRICK
AND TERRA-COTTA WORKS, ACCRINGTON

Garden Vases, etc.

434   435

436   437

Square   Square

ONE INCH SCALE.

Coal has been mined for local use in the area for centuries but it was not until the mid 19th century that the industry was commercially developed. At the 1841 census the third largest group of occupations after farmers and weavers was miners, but these worked in Altham rather than Huncoat. It was not until 1889 onwards that shafts were sunk to become Huncoat pit, one of the largest collieries run by Geo. Hargreaves & Co. whose proprietor was H. H. Bolton of Highbrake House. His son, Col. G.G.H.Bolton, followed his father in the business and later became Chairman of the N.W.Coal Board after the mines were nationalised in 1948. Access to the pit from Station Road was alongside Broad Meadows farm and over the railway bridge. The two winding gears are prominent with the upshaft in the foreground.

Henry Hargreaves Bolton

Geoffrey G. H. Bolton

Imagine a hole deep enough to hold one and a half Blackpool Towers with room to spare; or 3,500 Huncoat bricks laid on top of one another. That's how far under Huncoat these miners worked. A network of tunnels spread in all directions, connecting the colliery to other pits, and it was possible to walk underground from Scaitcliffe in Accrington, via Huncoat, to Calder Pit in Altham. Every year after the July holidays the manager had to walk this route for safety checks before the pit could restart.

The colliery had a record output in the 1950s of 1,300 tons in one day, and regularly hit its production targets. So regularly that the flags they were allowed to fly for hitting the target wore out.

When the pit closed in February 1968 there were still about a million tons of coal left, but it was not the sort consumers wanted and many geological faults made it uneconomical to work.

Above: A miner with one of the 15cwt tubs used to haul coal to the shaft. These had replaced earlier tubs of $3\frac{1}{2}$ cwt capacity. After nationalisation in 1948 the coal was hauled in three ton carts pulled by diesel locomotives.

Left: One of the diesel locos emerges from the gloom to cross the points, whilst a worker gets out of the way and takes a breather.

Below: On the surface were 150 coke ovens and extensive railway sidings where small saddle-tank engines shunted the coal and coke waggons ready to join the main line at Huncoat station.

The nearest Huncoat gets to having stately homes are the two manufacturers' mansions, Highbrake House and Woodside House. Highbrake had been built by Richard Fort in the late 18th century and was later for many years until 1848 the residence of Revd. Wm. Wood, the vicar of Altham, who also ran a school there for the sons of the more well-to-do local families. H. H. Bolton lived at Highbrake House before moving to North Wales in 1920 and it was later used as offices for the National Coal Board

IN PROUD MEMORY
OF THE MEN IN THE EMPLOY OF
GEORGE HARGREAVES & CO
THE COLLIERIES, ACCRINGTON
WHO GAVE THEIR LIVES IN THE GREAT WAR
1914 — 1919

Joseph Ainsworth
Harry Hargreaves Bolton
John Bolton
Henry Baron
Jack Bolton
William Edward Campion
Michael Cullen
James Duckworth
Sharples Parkinson Driver
Richard Eddleston
John Fort
Joseph Guilfoyle
Robert Wallace Hislop
James Heys
Percy Hope
Frank Heywood
John Thomas Hindle
Thomas Heys
Walter Hall
Benjamin George Hambling
Robert Hartley
Thomas Henry Jackson
Robert Jacques
John James Johnson
Myles Kirkman
George Keighley
Thomas Liggins
Fred Marsden
Ernest Mortimer
Thomas Ormerod
Joseph Prestage
William Stevenson
William Slinger
Ambrose Slinger
Henry Sherrock
Archibald Kitson Simpson
Peter Sumner
David Scholes
Albert Thompson
James Taylor
Ernest Wild
Frederick James Whittaker
George Worswick
Thomas Yates

Three of the four sons of H. H. Bolton were killed in the 1914-1918 war along with many of his employees. This memorial to forty four men of Accrington Collieries, including Huncoat pit, was moved from Highbrake House to St Augustine's Church in 1939.

Mr Bolton also donated generously, both privately and through his company, to the stained glass memorial window in the church which he and his remaining son unveiled in 1921. He was in great demand for unveiling memorials. He also officiated at the Huncoat and Oak Hill Park, Accrington, ceremonies.

Plans to replace the Accrington Corporation electricity works were first approved in 1946 and work started on a new power station off Altham Lane in 1948. The massive turbine house, chimneys and cooling towers towered 350 feet above the village, dominating the skyline and providing a landmark which could be seen for miles around. The station was coal fired and, along with the building, new railway sidings had to be constructed for shunting engines bringing wagonloads of coal from local collieries. A conveyor system delivered the coal to the top of the boiler house. The last load of coal from Huncoat pit was delivered in February 1968. In later years coal was brought by road from further afield. As coal supplies dwindled and collieries closed the power station became obsolete and shut down in 1984.

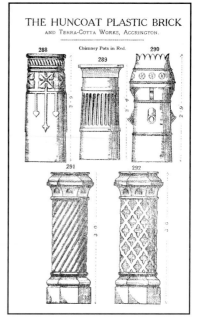

THE HUNCOAT PLASTIC BRICK
AND TERRA-COTTA WORKS, ACCRINGTON.

Chimney Pots in Red.

288 289 290

291 292

Early on a misty Sunday morning in October 1988 hundreds of spectators with almost as many cameras gathered on safe vantage points to watch as the cooling towers crumpled into dust. These were followed over the next two years by the chimneys and generating block in a succession of explosions. Within months ambitious plans were unveiled for the Zeri project, the dream of Stockport businessman Eddie Quigliotti. The site was to become a huge holiday complex with ski runs and water sports, pleasure park, arena and conference centre, hotel and lodges, monorail and cable car transport, much of it under glass in a temperature-controlled, year-round climate. Alas, the dream faded and the site remains undeveloped.

ZERI NEWS
The Huncoat Leisure Project

IT'S A WHOLE NEW WORLD...

How the national papers saw it:

My Disney World dream

Accrington may become the Venice of the North
THE GUARDIAN

Developer planning £300m theme park on mill town wasteland
Daily Mail

Accrington floated as Venice of the North
THE INDEPENDENT

Today Accrington, tomorrow the world
THE DAILY TELEGRAPH

The latest stage of Huncoat's industrial history began in 1957 when Accrington Council bought land between the railway and Whinney Hill to develop as an industrial estate. Critical voices were raised when the venture failed to attract new industry for several years. In 1971 Leonard Fairclough Ltd. opened the first works on the estate, manufacturing precast concrete beams for motorway bridges. These are now a familiar sight on Bolton Avenue and Burnley Road as they leave with a police escort for destinations around the country and all over the world. Slowly the estate began to fill with modern industrial units housing a variety of manufacturing and service industries.

Church and Chapel

Present day residents, accustomed to Huncoat's close association with Accrington, will think it odd that from very earliest times the township was part of Church Kirk parish. Not only were baptisms, marriages and funerals conducted *'over the hill and far away'*, but the parish was also responsible for poor relief, collection of rates and taxes, repair of highways, misbehaviour and a multitude of other civil matters. These duties were carried out by local parishioners appointed yearly, without payment, to the offices of churchwarden, overseer, constable and surveyor. During the nineteenth century these temporal duties were gradually transferred to local government bodies but Huncoat remained in the parish of St. James', Church Kirk until 1909. Even so, many Huncoat people chose to use Altham church to avoid the long and arduous walk over Whinney Hill, along Church Lane and Dill Hall to the parish church.

Before Henry VIII's dispute with the Pope in 1534, worship followed the Roman rite, but in succeeding centuries east Lancashire was staunchly Protestant. After 1559, those who stayed faithful to the old religion were forced to worship privately and secretly in family chapels such as those at Dunkenhalgh and Huncoat

Hall. Even after Catholics were freed from restrictions in 1829 it was still another hundred years before a Catholic church appeared in Huncoat.

Meanwhile, non-conformist beliefs had established a strong presence in the village. Baptists had started a Sunday school in 1807 followed by a chapel in 1810. After a shaky start in 1823 the Methodists gained a foothold by commencing their Sunday school in 1835. Even the then recently formed Mormon church is reported to have held recruiting meetings in the village in the 1840s.

In 1886 a Church of England mission room was opened on Brown Birks Lane, followed by the building of a church and the formation of Huncoat's own parish of St. Augustine in 1909. Perhaps because of its self-contained and rather isolated state, the village was obviously considered in need of salvation and ripe for missionary work. Each of the four denominations represented in the village was established as an offshoot of a distant church; the Baptists acknowledging their Accrington origin, the Methodists springing from Union Street, Accrington, St. Augustine's as a mission from St. James, Church Kirk and the Catholics from Sacred Heart, Accrington.

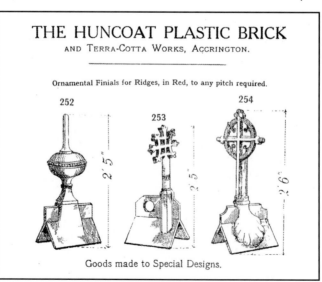

THE HUNCOAT PLASTIC BRICK

AND TERRA-COTTA WORKS, ACCRINGTON.

Ornamental Finials for Ridges, in Red, to any pitch required.

252   253   254

Goods made to Special Designs.

A window of the private chapel of the Birtwistle family at Huncoat Hall. During the years of Catholic persecution the chapel was served by priests trained abroad. Two of these, George Hothersall and Henry Kirkham, were reported to be *'lurking in Huncote'* in 1616. If found they would have been tried for treason and executed or imprisoned. Several sons of the Birtwistle family were educated at Douai College in northern France in the 16th and 17th centuries.

In January 1929 Fr. McAvoy of Sacred Heart began regular masses in Huncoat and soon after land was acquired for a chapel on Altham Lane near Stone Hey. Our Lady of Huncoat was opened in June 1931, served by priests from Sacred Heart. When St. Joseph's parish was formed in 1949 the chapel came under that church. In late 2003 it was announced that the chapel will close as part of a long term plan for Salford R.C. diocese.

...'until the past four years the village was destitute of any place of worship or means of religious instruction and its inhabitants sunk into a state of great ignorance and profaneness'. These were the words of William Perkins in 1810 when he appealed for donations towards the cost of a Baptist chapel. For a few years previous to this a small congregation of thirteen people had been meeting in a cottage at the side of the *White Lion* but had just erected a small meeting house next door at a cost of £200. This served as a chapel and Sunday school until 1875 except for five years in the 1840s when the minister was in dispute with his flock and refused to open the chapel. After the big influx of workers in the 1850s the building became too small and a larger school holding 300 was opened in 1875. This artist's drawing shows the three stages of growth; the original cottage, the plain chapel and the new school, from the entrance in Chapel Street alongside the *White Lion*. Even when this drawing was made in 1895 the new building had again become too small and plans were being discussed to celebrate the church's centenary in 1910 with a new building.

Fund raising efforts for an even grander Baptist edifice started in 1894 with a tea party. A plot of land adjacent to the school but fronting onto Burnley Lane was acquired and the first sod cut in April 1910. In May four hundred chapelgoers processed to the site to watch the laying of the six foundation stones.

George W. McAlpine wields the trowel as he prepares to declare the stone well and truly laid. In the following month he became Sir George.

With all six stones laid, the Mayor, stonelayers and other dignitaries pose for a group photograph following the ceremony. P.C.Walker keeps a watchful eye on the crowd. Little wonder with crowds this size that a second constable was appointed to the village in the following month! After the ceremony a meat tea was laid on in the Sunday School costing 9d for adults and 6d for children.

The official opening took place on Good Friday, 1911 by Sir G. W. McAlpine accompanied by John Barnes of Highbrake Mill, seen here mobbed at the church door by behatted ladies. The McAlpines lived at Broad Oak House and Mrs McAlpine insisted on having her letters addressed to – *Accrington, near Huncoat.*

The completed chapel towered over Burnley Lane, its massive frontage contrasting with the unpretentious stonework of the surrounding cottages. The high ground at the back caused continual problems with the rear wall and was partly the reason for its closure and demolition in 1966. Some of the foundation stones were later rescued and are built into a retaining wall in Spout House Lane

Sir George and Lady McAlpine

On the other side of the *White Lion* from the Baptist chapel was an old cotton warehouse. In 1835 the Methodists from Union Street, Accrington rented the top floor as a Sunday School. During the 1840s when the Baptist chapel was closed some of their followers joined the Methodists. The top floor room with its outside stairs became inadequate so a new school was built on Burnley Lane in 1844.

This in turn became too small and the present church and school building was erected at Stone Hey in 1869. At that time it stood in semi-isolation, with Broad Meadows farm the only other building between the church and the railway crossing.

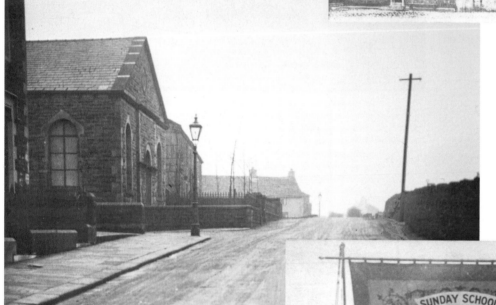

Methodist girls show off their banner with a painting of the church in this 1926 photograph.

St Augustine's Mission on Brown Birks Lane opened in 1886 as an offshoot of St James' Church at Church. Although dedicated to St Augustine of Hippo it was referred to locally as *'the church in the fields'* because of its position in what was then all farmland between Higher and Lower Brown Birks farms. Within Grove housing estate would not be built until over sixty years later. The lane became Bolton Avenue in 1948, named after the Bolton family, proprietors of collieries in Rossendale and Accrington

Work started on building the present church in 1908 followed by the dedication and opening on St Andrew's Day, November 30th, 1909. H. H. Bolton, colliery proprietor, of Highbrake House was a generous benefactor to the church. It's said that because his pit workings ran under the area a pillar of coal was left below the foundations of the church to prevent subsidence. In 1967 the parish was joined for a short time with St Margaret, Hapton and the following decade was a difficult period for the church. From September 1989 the parish combined with St John, Accrington. The original mission was sold and replaced in 1990 by Mapleford residential home for the elderly.

Whit Monday in Huncoat

When holidays were few, the Whit Monday processions of the churches were the highlight of Huncoat's year. Preparations began several weeks beforehand with the choosing of the music and, once the reluctance on the part of the young men had been overcome, start of rehearsals. The ladies were busy choosing, buying or making new dresses and hats. On Whit Sunday evening anxious eyes scanned the skies with a prayer for fine weather, all-important in Huncoat.

Monday morning was hustle and bustle as families donned their new clothes and rushed to be at the Sunday Schools by half past nine, ready to be marshalled for the start of the procession at ten o'clock. Friends and relatives not taking part lined the route and were joined by spectators from far and near attracted by the spectacle and no doubt by the chance to comment on the ladies' outfits. Each church walked separately in opposite directions but met at noon in front of the White Lion for a joint service and singing accompanied by a small group of musicians. The quality of the singing was a matter of friendly rivalry between the churches; sometimes the Methodists, sometimes the Baptists, being adjudged to have given the better performance.

Methodist Sunday School girls of 1925 are all dressed up with somewhere to go.

Not to be outdone the Baptists pause and pose at Highbrake Mill for their photograph.

48

Left: A ladies' procession passes Old Hall Farm on Highergate Road.

Below: Meanwhile the men struggle to keep the banner from lift-off.

Above: Starting the climb up Fish Lane in the 1920s.

Right: Some of these boys are rather ominously carrying violin cases – just as well this wasn't 1930s Chicago!

WHIT·MONDAY 1951.

1951. George Ormesher, Revd. McIver, Joseph Jaques and John J. Barnes lead the Baptist walk out of Towngate.

Guy Cunliffe conducts the singing in front of the *White Lion*.

Below: After the service the participants returned to their schools for coffee and buns and played games and sports on a nearby field until late in the evening. One lady recalled that her family always had brisket on the day and called it *'Whit Monday meat'*. On Whit Tuesday the Baptist choir went by wagonette to Holden, near Bolton-by-Bowland, for the annual picnic and had tea at the chapel there.

The combined Whit Monday walks managed to continue throughout the war years but by the 1950s changing social conditions were leading to a decline in church attendances and an end to the tradition in 1958. But the individual churches still held *walking days* on the occasion of Sunday School anniversaries or Rose Queen crownings for several more years.

Right: The Baptist ladies make one of their last walks along Burnley Lane in front of the chapel on a sunny Sunday in the 1960s.

The Last Time

HYMNS

To be sung by the Teachers and Scholars of the Baptist Sunday School, Huncoat, on Whit-Monday, May 26th, 1958.

HYMN I

Tune—*Duke Street*

JESUS shall reign where'er the sun
Does his successive journeys run;
His kingdom stretch from shore to shore
Till moons shall wax and wane no more.

Above: Part of the programme for the last combined Whit Walk.

Left: The Methodists reassemble at Towngate in 1988 after a short service on the green before making their way back along Lowergate Road to the church. Their final walking day took place in 1999.

Much of the entertainment in the village was provided by the various churches in the form of concerts, social evenings, field days, plays and tea parties.

A hundred years separate these two events and show the changed expectations and attitudes of the late twentieth century.

The Band of Hope was an organisation founded in 1855 with a mission to promote temperance amongst children. The evils of strong drink were pointed out to Sunday School classes and the children persuaded to *'sign the pledge'* not to partake of alcoholic drink. How many kept the pledge beyond teenage years is another question.

The Donkey Derby was a popular event during the incumbency of Father Lupton. The three times Grand National winner Red Rum appeared for several successive years. Another big attraction on a summer Sunday afternoon was the beer tent!

St. JOSEPH'S, ACCRINGTON

THE STEEL BAND

CHILDREN'S HOSPICE HOMELESS PROJECT

DONKEY DERBY 1993

PERSONAL APPEARANCE OF THE LEGENDARY

Red Rum
at Our Lady's, Altham Lane, Huncoat on Sunday 20th June, 1993

Gates Open 12 noon   First Race 1.00 p.m.

AMUSEMENTS GALORE   OFFICIAL RACE CARD: 50p

Other generous sponsors:-
MARCO LYSIUK, DARWEN, The Accrington Pipe Band
A & C ENGINEERING, NELSON, The Steel Band
DEPARTURE TRAVEL, ACCRINGTON, The P.A. System
EXPRESS GIFTS, Children's Entertainer
GEORGE .... ire

HUNCOAT
Baptist *Band of Hope.*

The Committee have pleasure in announcing that

On SATURDAY, October 1st, 1892,

A TEA PARTY AND
ENTERTAINMENT

Will be held in the SCHOOLROOM.

Chairman: Mr. FLOYD.   Speaker: Mr. SUTHERS.

PROGRAMME.

HYMN.	PRAYER.	CHAIRMAN'S ADDRESS.
SONG		Choir
	"Eawr Jack is off ageon,"	W. Pilkington
RECITATION		S. A. Booth
RECITATION	"Girls wanted,"	

Twenty five men of the village gave their lives in the First World War and six more in the Second World War. Many of them would have taken part in the Whit walks or attended social events in the various churches. On the 29th of April 1922 friends, relatives and neighbours gathered on the recreation ground to see the village war memorial unveiled by H. H. Bolton and dedicated by the Revd. J. B. Goodall, vicar of Huncoat. Prominent to the right of the picture within the railings is the bare-headed figure of Harold Peel, headmaster of Huncoat School and chairman of the Parish Council. In subsequent years Mr. Peel took the schoolchildren to the memorial each Remembrance Day to observe the two minutes silence.

IN MEMORY OF THE OLD SCHOLARS
OF
THE HUNCOAT
DAY AND EVENING SCHOOLS
WHO FELL IN DEFENCE OF
LIBERTY AND HONOUR
DURING THE GREAT WAR
1914-1918

W. ARMSTRONG   T. LIGGINS
J. BIRTWISTLE   J.W. METCALFE
R. BIRTWISTLE   T. MOBB
T. BOLTON   E. MORTIMER
W. FIELDS   W. NOWELL
J. FLOYD   H. RIDDLE
J. HEYS   F.W. RIDEHALGH
F. HEYWOOD   W. SEED
J.W. HURST   W. TAYLOR
J.J. JOHNSON   J.E. THORPE

Harold Peel himself unveiled the war memorial to the 20 boys of his school killed in the First War which was placed in the school hall in 1930. The old scholars subscribed to its cost and his son-in-law, John Holt, designed it. Four other names were added after the Second World War.

Mr Peel would not have been pleased when it was taken down and stored for many years until it was discovered and replaced outside the office in 1988.

Below: Three men connected with the Baptist Chapel were commemorated by a memorial organ, dedicated in 1922 by Miss Fields, daughter of one of the men. Here we see the start of the speech made on the occasion by Miss Fields, written by her own hand.

Dear Christian Friends,

I don't think you will expect a speech from me, but I must say you have conferred on me a great honour in appointing me to open this beautiful Memorial Organ.

This organ has been built as a memorial to the memory of my dear father, and his two friends Mr. Fred Ridehalgh and Mr. Thomas Liggins, all of whom fell in the Great War.

They were members of our Sunday School, and attended the services held in this Chapel. They gave their lives in the great cause of Freedom, and we are reminded of the words of the Saviour of men :- "Greater love hath no man than

A Residential Suburb

The latest stage of Huncoat's development commenced when the township amalgamated (was taken over?) with Accrington in 1929. At the customary tea party in the Town Hall one of the speakers remarked that he could quite imagine that in the very near future Huncoat would become the residential part of the Borough and he could visualise that soon all the best people would be living there instead of in Baxenden. Another speaker stated that one mile of main road would be added to Accrington, along which was some of the best building land in the borough.

Burnley Rural District Council didn't take kindly to the loss of Huncoat. At the handover its vice-chairman complained that they had spent £3,000 '...*making that road down there. Accrington couldn't expect to take it all in and give them 'nowt' for it after Burnley had laid out all that money'*.

The handover of deeds to the Mayor of Accrington in Huncoat School. The photographer forgot to ask them to say 'cheese'

By the end of the twentieth century Huncoat had indeed become a largely residential suburb of Accrington. All the old industries had disappeared and new ones confined in areas separate from housing. In the village, blocks of terraced housing filled the gaps on Station Road and Burnley Lane between the farms and old cottages. Several areas of council housing were developed from 1950 on. Good quality detached and semi-detached houses had spread along Burnley Road and Highergate Road. During the war temporary prefabricated dwellings filled the fields around St Augustine's church, to be replaced from 1948 on by the council housing estate at Within Grove. In the last decade of the century Foxwood Chase was built on the site of Burnley Road reservoir and Sutton Crescent replaced the fields between Spout House Lane and Burnley Road. In 2004 work started on another housing estate on the brickworks and mill site.

Left: New housing on Burnley Road.

Below: Highbrake and Prospect Terraces were one of the earliest housing developments, built to house workers at the nearby mill in the 1850s. They were unusual in being built as a crescent, perhaps trying to mimic the Regency grandeur of Buxton or Bath. For a time until 1968 the two end houses on the right were the Huncoat Workingmen's Club. Obviously five village pubs weren't enough for thirsty workers

STATION RD, HUNCOATS

Following the building of Prospect Terrace, Station Road began to be lined with houses and shops, starting with the *Railway Hotel* and progressing up the road to Stone Hey. Several of the terraces nearer the Methodist church have date-stones from the 1890s. The *Railway Hotel* was the last of the five public houses in Huncoat, opened in 1874 by Bentley's Milnshaw Brewery. This lower end of Station Road became the main shopping centre of the village in the mid 20th century. Up to a dozen small shops provided for the everyday needs of the villagers and the Co-op opened a large store next to the Methodist church in 1886. Only the Post Office, chip shop and newsagent remain.

Until the 1930s the road was almost cut in half by the barn of Broad Meadows farm, leaving only a narrow gap for vehicles between it and the cabins opposite.

Within Grove Estate Huncoat

After the end of World War 2 rows of *'prefabs'* were erected in the fields round St Augustine's church. These small bungalows were built to a standard design of mass produced panels bolted together on a concrete base. The estate was quickly christened *'Sawdust city'* because of the insulation used in the wall panels. The prefabs were later used for displaced persons and foreign workers before being demolished and replaced by the Burnley Road flats.

Welcomes You!

In 1948 Accrington Council began to develop the Within Grove housing estate. A waiting list and a points system meant that many families had a long wait to be allocated a council house. The whole estate has not had the best reputation despite many tenants taking the opportunity to become owner-occupiers and improve their homes. By the 1980s parts had become run down to the extent that it was used as the set for a film about conflict-torn Belfast. In 2003 large parts were cleared and await redevelopment.

At the start of the new millennium the prophesy of 1929 is coming true. Estates of superior quality houses have spread like a rash across the ancient farmlands and odd plots of land have been filled by smaller developments. There is a danger that the nature of a semi-rural community with large open spaces will be lost. The character of the village is also changing, with a commuting population that doesn't recognise the unique sense of identity felt by older Huncoaters. But echoes of the old independence and community spirit are still heard and will no doubt continue through the efforts of village clubs, councils and projects.

Left: Sutton Crescent and its satellite roads fill the fields between Highergate, Woodside Road and Spout House Lane.

High Class Grocer :: Orders Delivered

H. HEYS

FINEST DANISH BACON
FIRST CLASS PROVISIONS, PIES, CAKES,
FRUIT AND VEGETABLES
— Fresh Meat Daily —

★

8 WITHIN GROVE

"OUR AIM IS TO PLEASE"

Right: Burnley Road reservoir became redundant in the 1980s and was drained. Foxwood Chase estate was built on the site and, along with The Triangle, has connected Hillock Vale into the long ribbon of development along Burnley Road. As this book was prepared for press plans were announced for more house building at Hillock Vale.

The Dead End

For the past fifty years or more, Accrington has been exporting large numbers of its living into Huncoat. But the town has also been shipping its dead over the border for 140 years. In 1864 Accrington acquired 20 acres of land in Huncoat to lay out as a cemetery. These original acres have expanded to cover the old farm meadows from Whitewell Road to Bolton Avenue.

Until the opening of the cemetery most Huncoaters were buried at Altham or Church Kirk, with the cortege having to walk over Whinney Hill or down Altham Lane carrying the coffin. There was a small burial ground in front of the old Baptist Chapel but the only record of a burial there was this cast iron memorial to James Redman, designed by his son-in-law John Smith, who stands next to it.

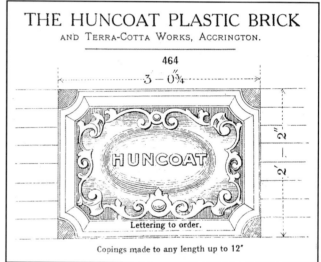

Other books about Huncoat include:

Old Homesteads of Accrington by Richard Ainsworth, 1928
History and Associations of Altham and Huncoat by Richard Ainsworth, 1932
Huncoat Remembered by John Smith, 1906 [reprinted 1985]
Huncoat Revisited by Jim Ashton, 2000
Within Grove: a memoir by Thomas G. Hargreaves, 2001

Copies of these can be found in Accrington Library.